My Disney
STARS AND HEROES 1

Student's Book with eBook

Tessa Lochowski

Scope and Sequence

Meet our Stars and Heroes!
page 4

	Character introductions	I'm …
	Hello, friends song	Hello

	Vocabulary	Grammar and communication	Personal and Social Capabilities	Cross-curricular	Project and strategies
1 **At school** page 10	**Classroom** Classroom objects 1 Classroom objects 2	**What's this? It's a backpack. Is it red? Yes, it is./No, it isn't.** *It's a ball. It's an orange eraser. Is it a blue book? Yes, it is./No, it isn't.* **Describe objects**	😊 **Self-awareness:** Identifying my emotions 1 *happy, sad, scared* **Story:** Let's play!	🌐 **Social Science:** My school day *circle time, class, lunch, recess*	📋 **Project:** Draw your classroom! **Self-management:** Getting ready for work *I'm ready!*
2 **Family and friends** page 22	**Family** Family and friends People and adjectives	**Who's this? This is Jess. She's my sister.** **Ask and answer about family** *He isn't my uncle. He's my dad. Is she your mom? Yes, she is./No, she isn't.*	😊 **Self-awareness:** Identifying my emotions 2 *excited, proud, worried* **Story:** The painting	🌐 **Social Science:** Family trees *baby, children, grandparents, parents*	📋 **Project:** My family tree **Presentation skills:** Introducing yourself, presenting your work *Hi! My name's … This is my …*
3 **Body and face** page 34	**Parts of the body 1** Parts of the body 2 Actions	*I have brown eyes. She has one nose.* **Give instructions** *Listen! Don't talk!*	😊 **Self-awareness:** Expressing my emotions 1 *cry, hide, jump, smile* **Story:** My monster	🌐 **Science:** Our five senses *hear, see, smell, taste, touch*	📋 **Project:** Design a monster **Self-management:** Good project work behavior *listen, open/close your books, sit down*
4 **Cool animals** page 46 	**Pets** Animals 1 Animals 2	*What's this? It's her dog. It's his hamster.* **Describe animals** *What are they? They're birds. What color are they? They're blue. Are they red? Yes, they are./No, they aren't.*	😊 **Self-awareness:** Expressing my emotions 2 *angry, frown, stomp, yell* **Story:** Good boy!	🌐 **Life Science:** Baby animals *chick, cub, foal, kitten, puppy*	📋 **Project:** My animal poster **Presentation skills:** Good presenter behavior *don't worry, smile, speak up, stand up*
5 **My things** page 58 	**Toys 1** Toys 2 Possessions	*I have a teddy bear. We don't have a ball. Do you have a kite? Yes, I do./No, I don't.* **Say what my friend has** *He has a train. She doesn't have a watch.*	😊 **Self-management:** Managing my emotions *close your eyes, count to ten, stomp your feet, take a breath* **Story:** Let's play!	🌐 **Technology:** Toys and materials *hard, plastic, plush, soft*	📋 **Project:** My things poster **Self-management:** Sharing and borrowing *Can I borrow an eraser, please? Yes, sure. Here you are.*

Welcome
page 6

Colors	What color is it?	It's red.	Relationship skills:
Numbers 1–20	Hello, my name's Mia. What's your name?	Hi! I'm Simon. Nice to meet you!	Welcoming new people to class
	How old are you? I'm six. Are you seven?	Yes, I am/No, I'm not.	Hi! Hello! Nice to meet you.

	Vocabulary	Grammar and communication	Personal and Social Capabilities	Cross-curricular	Project and strategies
6 **Food we like** page 70 	Food 1 Food 2 Food 3	I like pears and cheese. I like pears, too. I don't like carrots. **Ask and answer about likes and dislikes** Do you like cheese? Yes, I do!/No, I don't!	Social-awareness: Being nice to others *lonely, nice* Story: Let's have lunch!	Life Science: How tomatoes grow *grow, seed, soil, sunlight, water*	Project: My lunch plate **Presentation skills:** Good listener behavior 1 *clap hands, Good job! listen to others.*
7 **My free time** page 82 	Free time activities Activities 1 Activities 2	I can read. I can't sing. She can run. He can't dance. **Ask what my friends can do** Can you dance? Yes, I can./No, I can't. Can she dance? Yes, she can./No, she can't.	Self-management: Persistence *Don't give up. Go on! You can do it! It's hard. Keep trying* Story: Let's ride a bike!	Science: My body can move! *bones, joints, muscles, skeleton*	Project: 'About me' poster **Self-management:** Asking for help *Can you help me? How do you spell …?*
8 **My home** page 94 	Home Rooms and furniture Furniture and household items	Where's the rug? It's in the living room. **Describe where things are** There's a table. There are two chairs. There isn't a TV. There aren't any toys.	Responsible decision-making: Making decisions *I need … I don't need … Let's clean up! messy* Story: Where's the ball?	Design: Amazing houses *diamond, hexagon, oval, square*	Project: My dream bedroom **Presentation skills:** Good listener behavior 2 *ask questions, be polite, raise your hand, wait for your turn*
9 **Cool clothes** page 106	Clothes 1 Clothes 2 Personal possessions	I'm wearing jeans. I'm not wearing a dress. Are you wearing a dress? Yes, I am./No, I'm not. **Ask and answer about people's things** This is my bag. These are my books. Is this your bag? Yes, it is./No, it isn't. Are these your books? Yes, they are./No, they aren't.	Self-awareness: Feeling better *a hug, my favorite clothes, my favorite toy, my friend* Story: The lucky cap	Technology: Smart wool *cold, dry, hot, sheep, wet*	Project: My clothes poster **Self-management:** Planning your work *think and plan*

Picture dictionary pages 118–127   Stickers and Cut-outs

Meet our Stars and Heroes!

1 🎧 💬 Listen and point. Then point and say.

2 Collect your friend at the start of each unit!

Lightning McQueen — W
can
Friends: Mater and Sally

Riley — 1
can
Family: mom and dad

Violet — 2
can
Family: mom, dad, two brothers

Boo — 3
likes
Friends: Sully and Mike

Bolt — 4
likes
Friends: Penny and Rhino

Woody — 5
can
Friends: Buzz and Jessie

Remy 6 — friend — Likes: cheese

Rapunzel 7 — friends — Can: paint

Carl 8 — friends — Likes: his chair

Elsa 9 — can — Family: sister

Sing-along

3 🎵 Listen, sing, and act.

Hello, hello,
Say hello!
Say hello
To our friends and heroes!

4 ✏️ Be a hero. Draw and write.

Name: _____

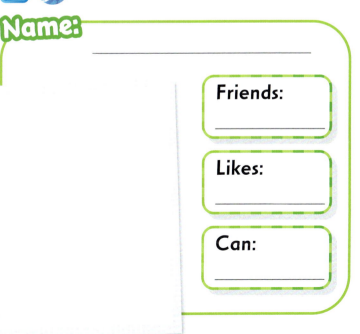

Friends: _____

Likes: _____

Can: _____

Welcome

LESSON 1 Colors

1 Listen, point, and say. Then ask a friend.

pink   brown   purple   orange   yellow   white

2 Watch the video. Circle and say.

3 Point and say.

What color is it?   It's red!

I can name colors.

gray

blue

LESSON 2 Greetings

1 Watch again. Circle. Who does Lightning meet?

2 Listen and say.

Hello, my name's Mia. What's your name?

I'm Simon.

Nice to meet you!

3 Listen, chant, and act. 🎵🎵

4 Now ask your friends.

I can introduce myself.

7

LESSON 3
Numbers

1 🎧 💬 Listen, point, and say. Then ask a friend.

1 one	2 two	3 three	4 four	5 five	6 six	7 seven
8 eight	9 nine	10 ten	11 eleven	12 twelve	13 thirteen	14 fourteen
15 fifteen	16 sixteen	17 seventeen	18 eighteen	19 nineteen	20 twenty

2 💬 Play a game with a friend.   Blue!   Five?   No!

3 ✏️ Stick. Then count, write the numbers, and circle.

three   eight   ten   twelve

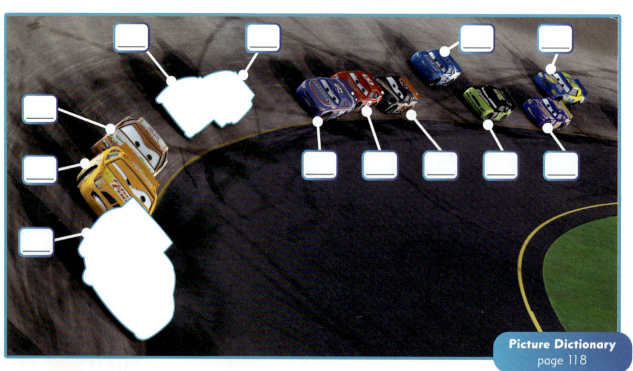

Picture Dictionary
page 118

8   I can say numbers 1–20.

Hello!

**LESSON 4
All about me**

1 🎧 **Listen and read. Who's seven today?**

Welcome new friends!

2 ✏️ 💬 **Draw and complete for you. Then ask a friend.**

Hello! My name's _____ .

Hi! How old are you?

I'm _____ .

I can give personal details.

LESSON 1 **Vocabulary**

3 🎧 1.1 💬 Listen, find, and say. Then ask a friend.

4 🎵 1.2 Listen, chant, and act. 🎵 🎶

student

desk

I can name people and things in my classroom.

Collect your friend! page 4

11

LESSON 2
Vocabulary

1 🎧 1.3 💬 Listen, point, and say. Then play.

Seven. Poster!

1. book
2. backpack
3. pencil
4. pen
5. chair
6. board
7. poster
8. door

2 🎧 1.4 💬 Listen and say. Then ask and answer.

Chair. What color is it?

It's yellow!

3 ✏️ Find and color. Then check (✔).

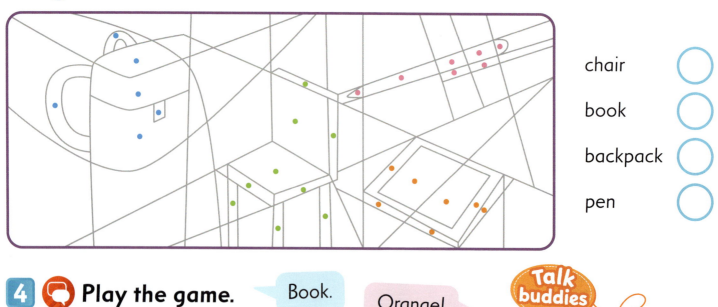

chair ⃝
book ⃝
backpack ⃝
pen ⃝

4 💬 Play the game.

Book.

Orange!

Talk buddies

12   I can name classroom objects.

LESSON 3
Grammar

1 🎧 ✏️ Listen and circle.

It's a **book** / **backpack**.

🎧 What's this?
It's a backpack.
Is it red?
No, it isn't.
Is it purple?
Yes, it is.

2 🎧 ✏️ Listen and stick. Then number.

Sticker time

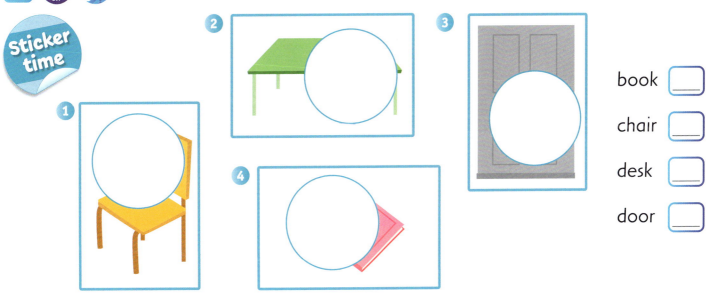

book ☐
chair ☐
desk ☐
door ☐

3 💬 Play *What's this?*

What's this? Is it red? Is it blue? It's a desk!

No, it isn't. Yes, it is.

Talk buddies

I can ask and answer about objects and colors.

**LESSON 4
Story**

Let's play!

1 🎧 1.8 Listen and read. Who's a good friend?

Spot! How many balls can you see in picture 4?

The end

2 ✏️ Look, read, and circle.

1. Who's a new student?

2. Who talks to Camila?

3. What do they play with?

3 ✏️ 💬 How does she feel? Follow, find, and say.

1. happy
2. sad
3. scared

4 💬 Act out the story.

Hi, I'm Li. Remember? Cool backpack!

Thanks.

Talk buddies

I can read and understand a story.

LESSON 5
Vocabulary

1 🎧 1.9 💬 Listen, point, and say. Then play.

1. crayon

2. eraser

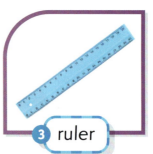
3. ruler

4. pencil case

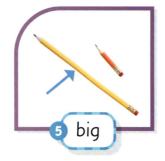
5. big

6. small

Make your own picture dictionary. Draw your school things.

Picture Dictionary page 119

2 🎧 1.10 💬 Listen and say. Then play in pairs.

It's green.

It's a crayon!

Sing-along

3 🎵 1.11 Listen, sing, and act.

Ready for school! Come and see!
Lots of fun in school for me.

It's a backpack.
It's big, it's blue.
With a big, brown book
And a small book, too.

Chorus

It's a pencil case.
It's small, it's red.
With a big, green ruler
And a small, pink eraser.

Chorus

16   I can name classroom objects and adjectives.   Extra Lesson   Go online Phonics

LESSON 6
Grammar and Speaking

1 🎬 ✏️ Watch the video. Color the balls.

🎧 1.12
It's a ball.   It's an eraser.
It's a yellow ball.   It's an orange eraser.
Is it a blue book?   Yes, it is./No, it isn't.

2 🎧 1.13 ✏️ Listen and number. Then say in pairs.

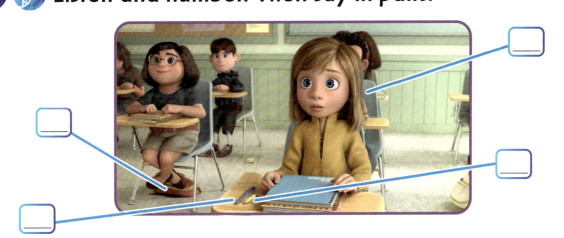

Let's communicate!

3 💬 Use the cut outs. Play the game.

Is it a green crayon?

Yes, it is!

I can describe objects.

17

LESSON 7
Myself and others

Listen and sing. 1.14

Happy, sad, scared

How are you?
How are you?
How are you today?

Are you **happy**?
Are you **sad**?
Are you **scared**?
How are you today?

Are you **angry**?
Are you **worried**?
Are you **excited**?
How are you today?

1 ✏️ **Look and circle. How do they feel?**

1 happy / sad   2 scared / happy   3 happy / scared   4 sad / happy

2 ✏️ 💬 **Draw for you. Then tell a friend.**

✨ Be a hero! ✨

Are you happy?
Make someone else happy too.

I'm _____. How are you?

18   Self-awareness I can say how I feel.

My school day

LESSON 8
My world

1   **Let's explore!** Listen and number.

The students are in the classroom. It's a **class**.

It's **circle time**.
Listen to the teacher.

It's **recess**.
Let's play!

It's **lunch**.
Yummy!

2   **Think** Read and match. Then say.

 a lunch   b recess   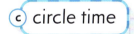 c circle time   d class

One.
It's a class.

3   **Do** What do you need for class? Check (✓). Draw one more.

I can read and understand about my school day.

LESSON 9
Project

Draw your classroom!

Let's review

1 ✏️ Read and number.

a

① It's my desk. It's my pencil case.

② It's my classroom. It's my teacher.

b

Get ready

2 🎧 ✏️ Listen and check (✓).
1.16

1. (pencil)
2. (ruler)
3. (eraser)
4. (paper plane)
5. (cookies)
6. (crayons)

I'm ready!

Workbook page 13

Create

3 🎨 Now draw your classroom. Write.

Reflect ☹ 🙂 😀

4 How did I do?

I have my things ready. ◯

I draw my classroom. ◯

I can draw and write about my classroom.

LESSON 10
Review

1 📝 💬 Look and number. Then say.

classroom ☐
poster ☐
student ☐
door ☐
chair ☐
board ☐

2 🎧 📝 Listen and color. Then read and circle.

① It's a **crayon** / **pen**.

② It's a **pencil** / **ruler**.

3 💡 Think and check (✓). Then stick!

I can ...
- 💬 name classroom things [ ]
- 📖 read a story [ ]
- 🎵 sing a song [ ]
- 🙋 say how I feel [ ]

Sticker time

✓ I completed Unit 1!

Go online
Big Project

21

LESSON 2
Vocabulary

1 🎧 2.3 💬 Listen, point, and say. Then play.

My family

1. big sister
2. baby brother
3. grandpa
4. grandma
5. aunt
6. uncle
7. cousin
8. friend

2 🎧 2.4 ✏️ Listen and number. Then circle.

 grandpa / grandma

 aunt / uncle

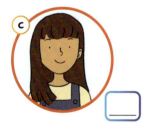 baby brother / big sister

 cousin / friend

3 💬 Play the game.

Mom.

Mom, grandma.

Mom, grandma, cousin.

Talk buddies

I can name family members.

24

LESSON 3
Grammar

1 🎧 2.5 Listen and check (✓).

This is Jack-Jack.

2 🎧 2.7 ✏️ Listen and stick. Then number.

Sticker time

 2.6
Who's this?
This is Oscar. He's my brother.
This is Jess. She's my sister.

a) He's my grandpa
b) She's my grandma.
c) She's my cousin.
d) He's my dad.

3 💬 Look at 2. Play *Who's this?*

Who's this?
Number three!

She's my cousin!
  Talk buddies

I can ask and answer about family.

25

LESSON 4
Story

The painting

1 🎧 2.8 **Listen and read. Whose family is it?**

Spot! Find five butterflies.

2 Look, read, and match.

1. brother   2. mom   3. grandma   4. grandpa

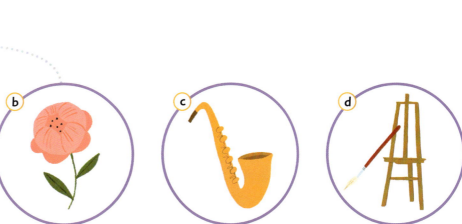

3 How do they feel? Find and check (✔).

1. He's excited. ○
   He's worried. ○

2. She's excited. ○
   She's proud. ○

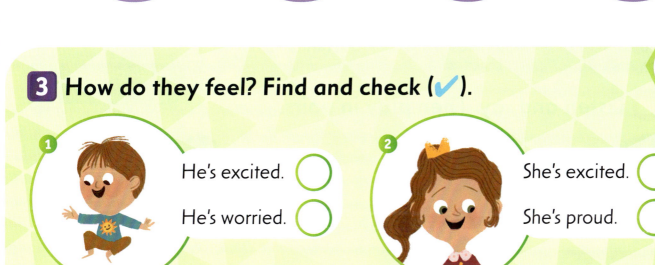

4 Act out the story.

This is my grandma.

Hello!

I can read and understand a story.

LESSON 5
Vocabulary

1 🎧 💬 Listen, point, and say. Then play.

1 boy

2 girl

3 young

4 old

5 nice

6 funny

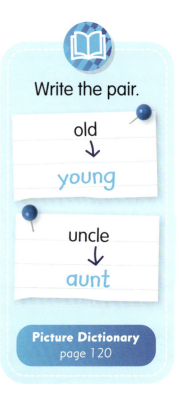

Write the pair.

old → young

uncle → aunt

Picture Dictionary page 120

2 🎧 💬 Listen and say. Then play in pairs.

 This is dad. He's …

Nice!

Sing-along

3 🎵 Listen, sing, and act.

*Family, family
This is my family.*

This is my grandma.
She's small. She's proud.
This is my grandpa.
He's old. He's funny.

Chorus

This is my dad.
He's big. He's nice.
This is my sister.
She's young. She's happy.

Chorus

I can describe people.

LESSON 6
Grammar and Speaking

1 Watch the video. Check (✓) Violet's friend.

He isn't my uncle.   He's my dad.
Is she your mom?   Yes, she is.
Is he your friend?   No, he isn't.

2 Listen and number. Then say in pairs.

a  b  c d

Let's communicate!

3 Use the cut outs. Talk in pairs.

Is he your cousin?   Yes, he is!

I can ask and answer about family.

29

LESSON 7
Myself and others

Listen and sing. 🎵 1.14

Excited, worried, proud

1 ✏️ Read and number. How do they feel?

a b c

1. She's proud.
2. She's worried.
3. He's excited.

2 💡 ✏️ How do you feel at these times? Color and say.

excited   proud   worried

1 2 3

Two. How do you feel?

I'm worried.

3 ✏️ 💬 Create an emoji. Say and act with a friend.

worried   proud   excited

Be a hero!

When are you proud? Think and say.

30   Self-awareness I can say how I feel.

Family trees

LESSON 8
My world
Social Science

1 🎧 2.14 ✏️ **Let's explore!**
Listen and number.

 a

① My sister, my brother, and I are **children**. My brother is a **baby**. He's young.

② My mom and dad are my **parents**.

 b

③ My grandma and grandpa are my **grandparents**. They're old.

 c

2 💡 ✏️ **Think** Put the words in order.

parents   grandparents   baby   children

young ← ⬚ — ⬚ — ⬚ — ⬚ → old

3 💬 **Do** Look and check (✔). Say in pairs.

grandparents ⭕
parents ⭕
children ⭕
baby ⭕

Grandma and grandpa.

Grandparents!

I can read and understand about family trees.

31

**LESSON 9
Project**

My family tree

Let's review

1 🎧 2.15 **Listen and check (✓).**

Get ready

2 🎧 2.16 ✏️ **Listen again and number in order.**

This is my … ☐   He's/She's … ☐

Hi, my name's … ☐

Workbook page 25

Create

3 🎨 💬 **Now make your family tree. Then tell the class.**

Reflect 😞 🙂 😄

4 How did I do?

I say my name. ○

I show my poster. ○

I use family words. ○

I can make and talk about my family tree.

32

LESSON 10
Review

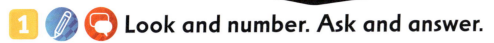

1 Look and number. Ask and answer.

mom ☐
friend ☐
brother ☐
dad ☐
big sister ☐

2 Look and circle. Then listen and check.

 Is she your grandma?
Yes, she is. / No, she isn't.

Is he your uncle?
Yes, he is. / No, he isn't.

 Is she your aunt?
Yes, she is. / No, she isn't.

3 Think and check (✓). Then stick!

I can ...

- name my family ◯
- read a story ◯
- sing a song ◯
- say how I feel ◯

Sticker time

✓ I completed Unit 2!

Go online
Big Project

33

3 Body and face

head

body

1 Watch the video. Check (✓).

LESSON 1 **Vocabulary**

2 Watch again. What do they do?

cry smile hide

3 Listen, find, and say. Then ask a friend.

4 Listen, chant, and act.

leg

arm

I can name the parts of my body.

Collect your friend!

LESSON 2
Vocabulary

1 🎧 3.3 💬 Listen, point, and say. Then play.

 1 face
 2 eye
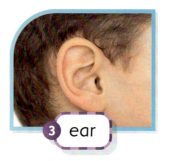 3 ear
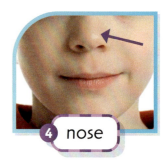 4 nose
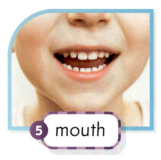 5 mouth
 6 hair
 7 hand
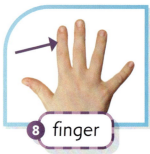 8 finger

2 🎧 3.4 💬 Listen and say Yes or No.

3 ✏️ Read and circle.
1. A pink **eye** / **mouth**.
2. Brown **hair** / **hands**.
3. Two **noses** / **ears**.
4. Ten **fingers** / **eyes**.

💡 one hand ➔ two hand**s**

4 💬 Play the game.

Two eyes. Yes!
Pink eyes. No!

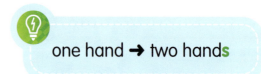

36 I can name parts of the body.

LESSON 3
Grammar

1   **Listen and number.**

I have two eyes!

I have brown eyes.
He has ten fingers.
She has one nose.

2   **Listen and stick. Then circle.**

She has gray
hair / nose.

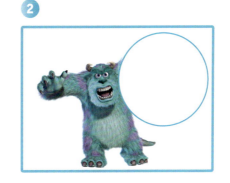

He has eight
hands / fingers.

She has one blue
mouth / eye.

3 **Play *Guess who?***

She has purple hair.

Three!

I can give basic descriptions of people.

LESSON 4 — Story

My monster

1 🎧 3.8 Listen and read. Who helps Hugo?

Spot! Can you find two eyes the same?

The end

2 ✏️ Look, read, and match.

1. He has two eyes.
2. He has four legs.
3. He has three legs.
4. She has four arms.

a    b    c    d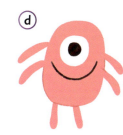

3 ✏️ How does Hugo feel? Circle.

1.  I'm **sad** / **excited**.
2.  I'm **worried** / **happy**.

4 💬 Act out the story.

Oh no! His eye! He only has one eye!

Are you OK?

Talk buddies

I can read and understand a story.

LESSON 5
Vocabulary

1 🎧 💬 Listen, point, and say. Then play.

1. sit down

2. stand up

3. listen

4. show

5. open

6. close

One word or two words?

one word
listen

two words
sit down

Picture Dictionary page 121

2 🎧 💬 Listen and do. Then play in pairs.

 Stand up!

Sit down!

Sing-along

3 🎵 Listen, sing, and act.

Listen, listen,
Listen to the music.
Follow me.
One, two, three!

Stand up!
Show your hands!
Jump in the air!
Sit down on your chair!

Chorus

Close your eyes!
Touch your head!
Open your eyes!
Stand up again!

Chorus

I can name actions.

LESSON 6
Grammar and Speaking

1 Watch the video. Circle. What does Sully do?

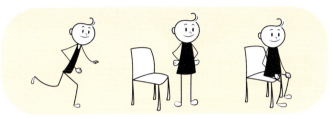

Listen! Don't talk!
Stand up! Don't sit down!

2 Listen and check (✔). Then say in pairs.

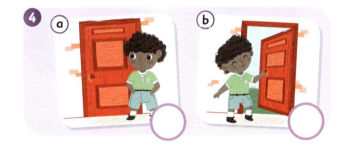

Let's communicate!

3 Use the cut outs. Play the game.

Open your eyes!

I can give instructions.

41

LESSON 7
Myself and others

Expressing emotions

 Listen and sing. 1.14

1 Think and say. How do they feel?

 cry

 hide

 jump

 smile

2 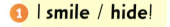 Listen and circle. Then say and act.

1. I smile / hide!

2. I jump / cry!

3. I smile / hide!

4. I hide / jump!

I'm happy.

I smile!

3 Match and say.

Be a hero!

Can you make your friend smile in 30 seconds? Try making a funny face.

42   Self-awareness   I can name actions and emotions.

Our five senses

 LESSON 8
 **My world**

1   **Let's explore!** Listen and number.

I **see** with my eyes. I see colors – red, blue, orange, and green.

I **hear** with my ears. I hear music.

I **smell** with my nose. I smell the flowers.

I **taste** with my mouth. I taste my lunch. Yum!

I **touch** with my fingers. I touch the water. It's wet!

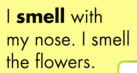

2   **Think** Look and match.

1 see   2 hear   3 touch   4 taste   5 smell

a   b   c   d   e

3   **Do** Think and say. Draw one more.

I see…

I can read and understand about my senses.

43

LESSON 9
Project

Design a monster

Let's review

1 ✏️ Read and write the number.

1. This is my monster. He has _____ arms.

2. This is my monster. She has _____ eye.

Get ready

2 🎧 3.16 ✏️ Think and circle. Then listen and check.

Sit down! / Stand up!

Listen! / Don't listen!

Open / Close your books.

Workbook page 37

Create

3 🎨 Now design your monster. Write.

Reflect ☹ 🙂 😀

4 How did I do?

I listen to my teacher. ⭕

I get my pencils ready. ⭕

I create my monster. ⭕

44

I can design and write about my monster.

LESSON 10
Review

I can do it!

1 Look and number. Then say.

eye ☐   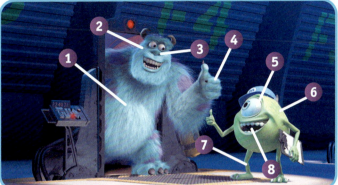   leg ☐
face ☐   body ☐
finger ☐   nose ☐
head ☐   mouth ☐

2 Write *a* or *b*. Then listen and check.

a

1. He has one eye. ____
2. She has purple hair. ____
3. He has two arms. ____
4. She has six legs. ____

b

3 Think and check (✓). Then stick!

I can ...
- name body parts and actions ☐
- read a story ☐
- sing a song ☐
- name actions and emotions ☐

Sticker time

✓ **I completed Unit 3!**

Go online
Big Project

45

4 Cool animals

Video story

bird

1 Watch the video. Check (✓).

LESSON 1 **Vocabulary**

2 Watch again. How does Rhino feel?

excited   angry   scared

3 Listen, find, and say. Then ask a friend.

4 Listen, chant, and act.

dog   hamster   cat

I can name animals.

Collect your friend!

LESSON 2
Vocabulary

1 🎧 💬 Listen, point, and say. Then play.

 1 mouse
 2 fish
 3 rabbit
 4 frog
 5 turtle
 6 lizard
 7 snake
 8 horse

2 🎧 💬 Listen and check (✓) in 1. Then play in pairs.

It's small. It's gray.   A mouse!

3 ✏️ Join the dots and circle. Then color.

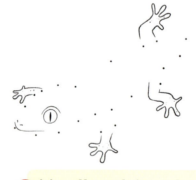

1 It's a **turtle** / **mouse**.   2 It's a **lizard** / **snake**.   3 It's a **frog** / **fish**.

4 💬 Play the game.

Is it big?   Yes, it is.

Is it white?

Talk buddies

I can describe animals.

48

LESSON 3
Grammar

1 🎧 4.5 ✏️ Listen and circle.

🎧 4.6
What's this?
It's her dog.
What's this?
It's his hamster.

It's her **dog** / **mouse**!

2 🎧 4.7 ✏️ Listen and stick. Then write.

① It's her _____ .
② It's his _____ .
③ It's her _____ .
④ It's his _____ .

3 💬 Play *What's this?*

What's this?

It's her rabbit.

I can say whose animal it is.

49

LESSON 4
Story

Good boy!

1 🎧 4.8 Listen and read. What's Emma's toy?

Spot! Can you find six birds?

The end

2 ✏️ **Look, read, and circle.**

1. Buddy is her dog.

2. Emma has this toy.

3. The children think Buddy is

3 How does Emma feel? Look and check (✔).

1.  She's happy. ◯
   She's angry. ◯

2.  She's proud. ◯
   She's worried. ◯

4 💬 **Act out the story.**

 Thank you, Buddy! Good job!

 He's a cool dog!

I can read and understand a story.

51

LESSON 5
Vocabulary

1 🎧 💬 Listen, point, and say. Then play.

 1 duck
 2 fox
 3 squirrel

 4 spider
 5 ant
 6 bee

Which animals have four legs?

fox

Picture Dictionary
page 122

2 🎧 💬 Listen and say. Then play in pairs.

 It's small. It's black and brown.

Ant!

Sing-along

3 🎵 Listen, sing, and act.

Look, they're ducks.
They're green and gray.
Look, they're squirrels.
They jump and play.

*Animals! Animals!
Look at the animals!*

Look, they're spiders.
They're small and brown.
Look, they're ants.
They run around.

Chorus

I can name animals.

Extra Lesson

Go online
Phonics

52

LESSON 6
Grammar and Speaking

1 Watch the video. Check (✓). What animals can you see?

4.12
What are they?	They're birds.
What color are they?	They're blue.
Are they red?	No, they aren't.
Are they gray?	Yes, they are.

2 4.13 Listen and number. Then write and say in pairs.

Five. What are they?   They're _____ .

Let's communicate!

They're horses.   What color are they?

3 Use the cut outs. Play the game.

They're brown. They're a pair!

I can ask and answer about animals.

53

LESSON 7
Myself and others

Expressing anger

Listen and sing. 🎵 1.14

1 ✏️ **Look and act. Then circle.**

 frown

 stomp

 yell

They're...
worried
angry
excited

2 🎧 4.14 ✏️ **Listen and number. Then act.**

 a

 b

 c

I'm angry.

It's OK.

3 💡 **Which body part do you use? Circle.**

	a	b	c
1 Yell			
2 Stomp			
3 Frown			

Be a hero!

When you're angry, curl up into a ball and frown!

Self-awareness I can name actions and emotions.

54

Baby animals

 LESSON 8
My world

1   **Let's explore!** Listen and number.

It's a baby fox.
It's a **cub**. ☐

It's a baby cat.
It's a **kitten**. ☐

It's a baby bird.
It's a **chick**. ☐

It's a baby dog.
It's a **puppy**. ☐

It's a baby horse.
It's a **foal**. ☐

2 **Think** Read and circle.

1 A **kitten** / **puppy** is a baby dog.

2 A **cub** / **foal** is a baby horse.

3 A **kitten** / **chick** is a baby cat.

4 A **cub** / **puppy** is a baby fox.

5 A **foal** / **chick** is a baby bird.

3 **Do** Draw the baby animals. Then write.

It's a _____ .

It's a _____ .

I can read and understand about baby animals.

55

LESSON 9
Project

My animal poster

Let's review

1   **Listen and number.**

b. This is a rabbit. It's white. It has big ears.

a. This is a squirrel. It's small and orange. It's funny.

Get ready

2   **Listen and circle.**

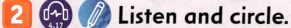

 Stand up!

 Frown.

 Speak up.

 Smile!

Workbook page 49

Create

3 Now make your poster. Then tell the class.

Reflect

4 How did I do?

I stand up.

I talk about my animal.

I speak up.

I smile.

I can make and present my animal poster.

I can do it!

LESSON 10
Review

1 ✏️ 💬 Look and circle. Ask in pairs.

What color is it?

① fox / bird   ② cat / fish   ③ horse / hamster

2 🎧 4.18 Listen and check (✓). Then write.

①

②

They're _____ .   They're _____ .

③

④

_____ .   _____ .

3 💡 Think and check (✓). Then stick!

I can ...

- 💬 name animals ☐
- 📖 read a story ☐
- 🎵 sing a song ☐
- 👤 name actions and emotions ☐

Sticker time

✓ I completed Unit 4!

Go online
Big Project

57

5 My things

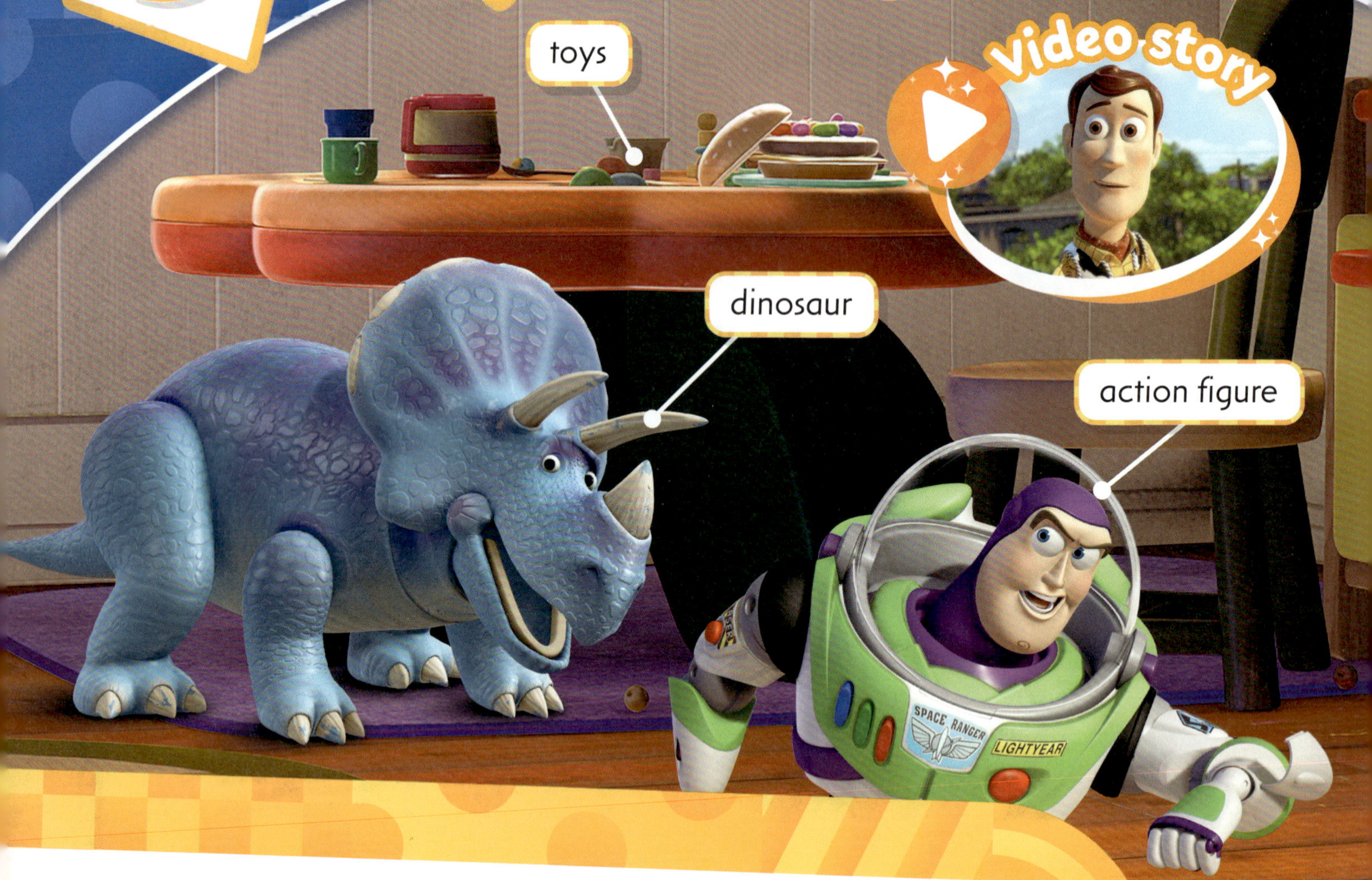

toys
Video story
dinosaur
action figure
SPACE RANGER
LIGHTYEAR

1 5A **Watch the video. Check (✔).**

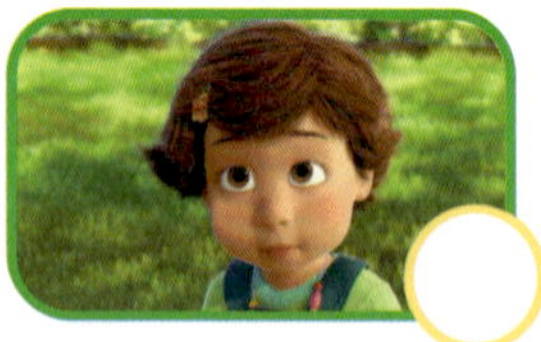

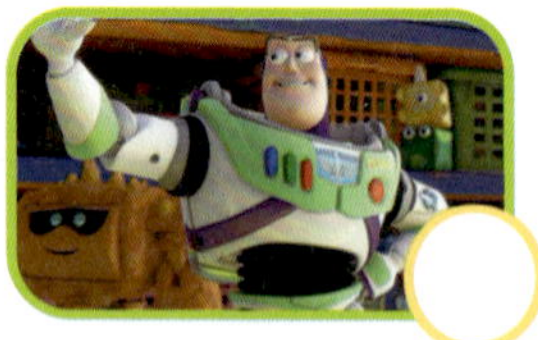

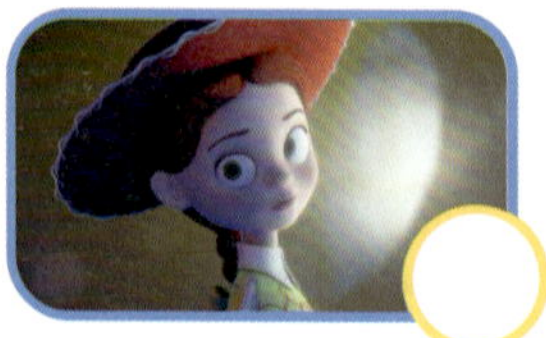

2 5A **Watch again. What does Woody do?**

close your eyes

stomp

take a breath

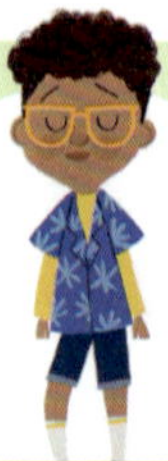

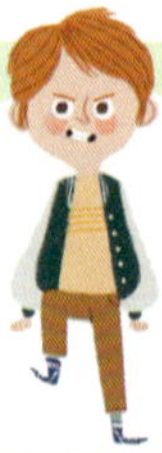

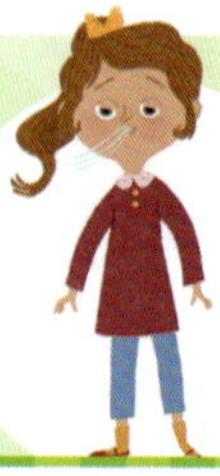

LESSON 1 **Vocabulary**

3 🎧 💬 Listen, find, and say. Then ask a friend.

4 🎵 Listen, chant, and act. 🎵 🎵

doll

I can name toys.

Collect your friend!

59

LESSON 2
Vocabulary

1 🎧 5.3 💬 Listen, point, and say. Then play.

1. ball

2. train

3. car

4. plane

5. robot

6. teddy bear

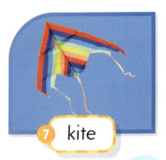
7. kite

8. new

2 🎧 5.4 ✏️ Listen and match.

💡 new ➜ old

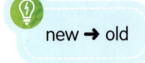

3 ✏️ Look at 2. Circle.

1. I have a new **car / robot**.
2. I have an old **plane / train**.

4 💬 Play the game.

A new robot. — Yes!

An old train. — No!

Talk buddies

60 — I can name and describe toys.

**LESSON 3
Grammar**

1 🎧 5.5 **Listen and check (✓).**

🎧 5.6
I have a teddy bear. I don't have a train.
We have an action figure. We don't have a ball.
Do you have a kite? Yes, I do. / No I don't.

We have an action figure.

2 🎧 5.7 ✏️ **Listen and stick. Then write.**

  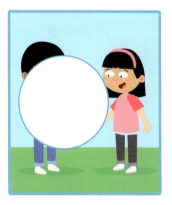 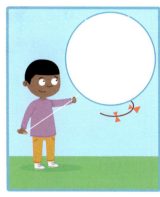

① I have a _____.
② We have a _____.
③ We have a _____.
④ I have a _____.

3 💬 **Play Guess who?**

Do you have a robot?

Number one!

Yes, I do.

Talk buddies

I can say what I have.

61

LESSON 4 Story

Let's play!

1 🎧 5.8 Listen and read. Who's angry?

Spot! Can you find three different cars?

The end

2 Look, read, and circle.

1. What toy does Arjun's brother have?
   a    b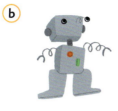

2. Who wants the robot?
   a    b

3. How does Arjun feel?
   a    b

4. Who helps Arjun and his brother?
   a    b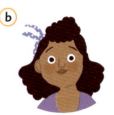

3 How does Arjun calm down? Think and check (✓).

…seven, eight, nine, ten!

4 Act out the story.

Hey! That's my robot!

No, it's my robot!

Talk buddies

I can read and understand a story.

LESSON 5
Vocabulary

1 🎧 5.9 💬 Listen, point, and say. Then play.

1 tennis racket

2 tablet

3 TV

4 watch

5 scooter

6 board game

One word or two words?

one word
tablet

two words
board game

Picture Dictionary
page 123

2 🎧 5.10 💬 Listen and say. Then play in pairs.

It's big.

It's a scooter!

Sing-along

3 🎵 5.11 Listen, sing, and act.

Toys, toys, toys!
I have toys.

I have a scooter.
It's red and it's new.
I have a teddy bear.
I have a board game, too.

I don't have a tablet
Or a big TV,
But I have an action figure
And some robots,
One, two, three.

Chorus

I can name my things.

64

LESSON 6
Grammar and Speaking

1 Watch the video. Circle the toys Bonnie has.

> She has a horse. She doesn't have a tablet.
> He has a train. He doesn't have a watch.

2 Look and check (✓). Listen. Then say in pairs.

- tennis racket ◯
- doll ◯
- kite ◯
- toy horse ◯
- dinosaur ◯
- board game ◯

> She has a dinosaur.

> She doesn't have a board game.

Let's communicate!

3 Use the cut outs. Play the game.

> He has a scooter.

> She doesn't have a scooter.

I can say what my friend has.

65

LESSON 7
Myself and others

Listen and sing. 🎵 1.14

Managing emotions

1 How do they feel? What can they do?

2 🎧 5.14 ✏️ Listen and write 1 or 2. Then say for you.

a
b
c

When I'm angry, I _____ .

3 Check (✔). What can you do next time you need to calm down?

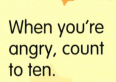

Be a hero!

When you're angry, count to ten.

...4, 5, 6...

Self-management I can manage my emotions.

Toys and materials

 **LESSON 8 My world**

1 **Let's explore!** Listen and number.

Look at my toys! I have a plush teddy bear and some plastic dolls.

My robot isn't soft. It's **plastic**. My tablet is plastic, too. They're **hard**.

This is my teddy bear! It's **plush**. My toy dinosaur is plush, too. They're **soft**.

2 **Think** Look and match. Then say in pairs.

1

2

 IT'S HARD.
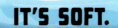 IT'S SOFT.
 IT'S PLASTIC.
 IT'S PLUSH.

3

4

3 **Do** Look and say. Then complete.

 It's hard.   It's soft.

I can read and understand about materials.

LESSON 9 Project

My things poster

Let's review

1 Look and check (✓).

1. I have a plane. I don't have a tablet. ○
2. I have a robot and a board game. I don't have a kite. ○

Get ready

2 🖊 🎧 5.16 Look, circle, and write. Then listen and check.

I have a pencil. I don't have an eraser. Can I borrow an _____ , please?

Yes, sure. Here you are.

Thank you!

Workbook page 61

Create

3 🎨 Now make a poster about your things. Write.

Reflect

4 How did I do?

I have what I need.

I ask to borrow things.

I share with my friends.

I can make a poster and write about my things.

**LESSON 10
Review**

I can do it!

1 📝 💬 **Look and number. Then say.**

a
b
c 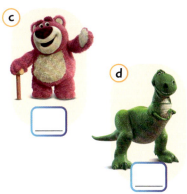 (c and d)
d
e

1. action figure
2. toy horse
3. dinosaur
4. teddy bear
5. doll

2 📝 🎧 **Write. Then listen and check.**
5.17

car   doll   train   action figure

1. He has a _____ .
2. He has an _____ .
3. He doesn't have a _____ .
4. He doesn't have a _____ .

3 💡 **Think and check (✓). Then stick!**

I can ...
- 💬 name my toys and things ☐
- 📖 read a story ☐
- 🎵 sing a song ☐
- 🌈 manage my feelings ☐

Sticker time

✓ **I completed Unit 5!**

Go online
Big Project

69

6 Food we like

cheese

bread

1 ▶ Watch the video. Check (✔).

LESSON 2
Vocabulary

1 🎧 💬 Listen, point, and say. Then play.

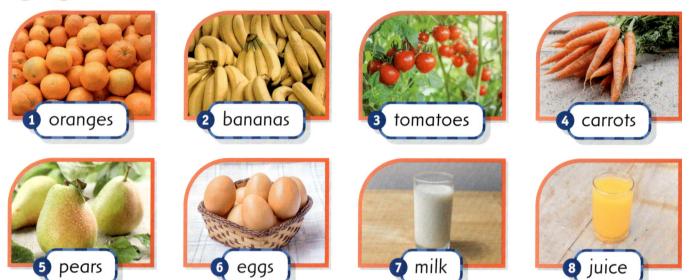

1. oranges
2. bananas
3. tomatoes
4. carrots
5. pears
6. eggs
7. milk
8. juice

2 ✏️ 🎧 Join the dots and check (✓). Then listen and say Yes or No.

carrots ○   onions ○
bananas ○   bread ○
eggs ○   oranges ○
juice ○   tomatoes ○

3 💬 Choose three things for lunch. Then guess.

Talk buddies

Pears?
No!
Carrots?
Yes!

I can name food and drinks.

LESSON 3
Grammar

1 🎧 6.5 Listen and check (✓).

I like bread and grapes, too.

🎧 6.6
I like pears and cheese.
I like pears, too.
I don't like carrots.

2 🎧 6.7 ✏️ Listen and stick. Then write.

I don't like _____ .

I like milk and _____ .

3 💬 Say and play.

I like milk.

I like milk, too!

I can say what food I like and don't like.

73

LESSON 4
Story

Let's have lunch!

1 🎧 6.8 Listen and read. Who do the children help?

Spot! Can you see fish?

2 ✏️ Look, read, and match.

1. He has bananas.
2. She has carrots.
3. She has grapes.
4. He has eggs.

 a
 b
 c
 d

3 Read, think, and check (✓).

1. How does Alicia feel?

 a  b

2. What does Camila do?

 a  b

3. How do they feel at the end?

 a  b

4 💬 Act out the story.

Can we help?

Let's go and talk to her!

Talk buddies

I can read and understand a story.

LESSON 5
Vocabulary

1 🎧 💬 Listen, point, and say. Then play.

 1 pie
 2 pasta
 3 rice
 4 meat
 5 jam
 6 fruit

Think and write.

Food I like:
fruit
Food I don't like:
meat

Picture Dictionary page 124

2 🎧 💬 Listen and say. Check (✓) in 1. Then play in pairs.

 I like rice.

I like rice and meat.

Sing-along

3 🎵 Listen, sing, and act.

I like pie
And I like cheese.
I like rice
But I don't like meat.

Yes, I like rice
But I don't like meat.

I like pasta.
And jam is good.
I like fruit
But I don't like juice.

Yes, I like fruit
But I don't like juice.

76

I can name food. Extra Lesson

Go online Phonics

LESSON 6
Grammar and Speaking

1 Watch the video. Circle. What does Remy like?

Do you like cheese?　　Yes, I do.
Do you like tomatoes?　　No, I don't.

2 Listen and put a ✔ or ✘. Then ask a friend.

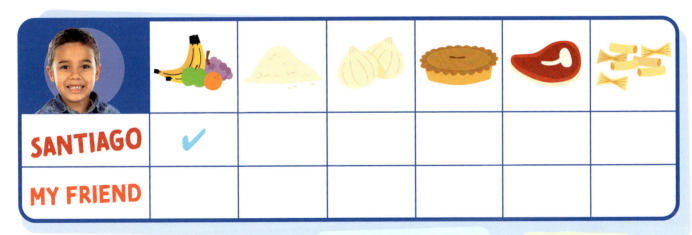

Do you like fruit?　　No, I don't.

Let's communicate!

3 Use the cut outs. Play the game.

I like pasta. Do you like pasta?

Yes, I do. Do you like juice?

No, I don't.

I can ask and answer about likes and dislikes.

LESSON 7
Myself and others

Be nice to others

Listen and sing. 1.14

1 Who's lonely? Circle in green. Who's nice? Circle in blue.

a　b　c　d

2 Think and check (✓). Then act.

Come and play with us!
1

This is fun!
2

Are you OK? Can I help?
3

3 How can you be nice? Check (✓) and draw.

Be a hero!
How can you be nice this week? Keep a diary.

Social awareness I can be nice to others.

How tomatoes grow

LESSON 8
My world

1   **Let's explore!** Listen and number.

The tomato plants are small. Give them **water** and **sunlight**.

The tomato plants **grow**!

Tomatoes are fruit. They have **seeds**.

The tomatoes are big now. You can eat them!

Put the seeds in the **soil**.

2  **Think** Look and circle.

It has seeds.
pear cheese grape
orange carrot

It grows.
baby puppy kitten
car book

3   **Do** Number. Then say.

1  → 2  → 3  → 4  → 5

soil ☐   water ☐   sunlight ☐   grow ☐   seeds ☐

I can read and understand about how things grow.

79

**LESSON 9
Project**

My lunch plate

Let's review

1 🎧 6.15 **Listen and check (✓).**

I don't like pie. I like rice and carrots.

I like pasta and juice. I like fruit.

Get ready

2 🎧 6.16 ✏️ **Circle. Then listen again and check.**

1 a   b
2 a   b

Workbook page 73

Create

3 🎨 💬 Now design your lunch plate. Then tell the class.

Reflect 😟 🙂 😄

4 How did I do?

I listen to others. ○

I clap my hands. ○

I say *Good job!* ○

I can make and present my lunch plate.

LESSON 10
Review

I can do it!

1 ✏️ 💬 Circle. Then say for you.

1. eggs / pears
2. jam / onions
3. grapes / bread
4. meat / pasta

I like pears.   I don't like eggs.

2 🎧 ✏️ Listen and number. Then ask and answer.
6.17

Do you like bananas?
Do you like oranges?

No, I don't.
Yes, I do.

3 💡 Think and check (✓). Then stick!

I can ...

- 💬 name food and drinks
- 📖 read a story
- 🎵 sing a song
- 🧍 be nice to others

sticker time

✅ **I completed Unit 6!**

Go online
Big Project

7 My free time

read

play the guitar

LESSON 1 **Vocabulary**

1 Watch the video. Check (✓) Rapunzel's friends.

2 Watch again. How does Rapunzel feel?

excited
happy
sad
angry
scared

3 Listen, find, and say. Then ask a friend.

4 Listen, chant, and act. 🎵 🎵

paint

dance

I can name free time activities.

Collect your friend!

LESSON 2
Vocabulary

1 🎧 💬 **Listen, point, and say. Then play.**

 1 run
 2 ride a bike
 3 throw a ball
 4 catch a ball
 5 sing
 6 play soccer
 7 play video games
 8 jump rope

2 🎧 💬 **Listen and say. Then say and do.**

Sing!

3 💡 ✏️ **Think and match.**

1   2   3   4   5   6

a play video games   c run   e throw a ball
    b jump rope   d ride a bike   f play soccer

4 💬 **Act and guess.**

Catch a ball!

Talk buddies

I can name free time activities.

LESSON 3
Grammar

1 Look and circle. Then listen and check.

I can read.
I can't sing.
She can run.
He can't dance.

She can **read** / **play video games**.

2 Listen and stick. Then circle and say.

She can paint.   He can't run.

1
She **can** / **can't** play the guitar.

2
She **can** / **can't** paint.

3
He **can** / **can't** ride a horse.

4
He **can** / **can't** run.

3 Write about you. Then tell a friend.

I can _____ .   I can't _____ .

I can say what people can and can't do.

85

LESSON 4
Story

Let's ride a bike!

1 🎧 7.8 Listen and read. Who helps Camila?

Spot! Find three robots.

2 ✏️ Look, read, and write Yes or No.

 Camila can ride a bike. _____

 Li can help. _____

 Camila is scared. _____

 Her friends are angry. _____

3 ✏️ What do Camila's friends say? Circle.

 Go on! You **can** / **can't** do it!

 Keep **crying** / **trying**!

 Don't **give up** / **stand up**!

4 💬 Act out the story.

I'm scared! I can't do it!

Yes, you can!

Talk buddies

I can read and understand a story.

LESSON 5
Vocabulary

1 🎧 7.9 💬 Listen, point, and say. Then play.

 1 swim
 2 draw
 3 hop
 4 bounce a ball
 5 play the piano
 6 use a computer

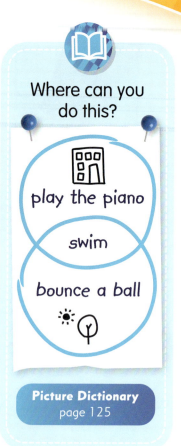

Where can you do this?
- play the piano
- swim
- bounce a ball

Picture Dictionary page 125

2 🎧 7.10 💬 Listen and say. Then play in pairs.

 I can …

… draw!

Sing-along

3 🎵 7.11 Listen, sing, and act.

I can use a computer.
I can bounce a ball.
I can't play the piano
And I can't draw.

I can swim.
I can hop, hop, hop.
One, two, three.
Can you hop with me?

I can name free time activities.

Extra Lesson

Go online Phonics

LESSON 6
Grammar and Speaking

1 Watch the video. Circle. Who helps Rapunzel?

Can you dance?   Yes, I can.
Can she dance?   Yes, she can.
Can he dance?   No, he can't.

2 Listen and put a ✔ or ✘. Then ask and answer.

	Finn	Esther
dance		
bounce a ball		
sing		
play the piano		

Can he dance?

Yes, he can.

Can he sing?

No, he can't.

Let's communicate!

3 Use the cut outs. Play the game.

I can paint. Can you paint?

Yes, I can!

I can ask what my friends can do.

89

LESSON 7
Myself and others

Keep trying!

Listen and sing. 🎵 1.14

1 💡 Think. How do Rapunzel and Camila feel? What new things do they do?

2 🎧 7.14 ✏️ Listen and number.

3 💡 ✏️ Put a ✓, ✗, or ★ for you. Draw one more.

I can do it! ✓   I can't do it. ✗   I keep trying. ★

Be a hero!
Try to learn something new. Don't give up!

Self-management I can show persistence.

My body can move!

LESSON 8
My world

1   **Let's explore!** Listen and number.

And I have **muscles**. They help my bones and joints move.

Look! I can jump! And I can run! But how can my body move?

I have **bones** in my body. This is my **skeleton**.

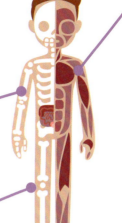

I have **joints** between my bones.

My body works hard when I run and jump!

2   **Think** Check (✔) who is moving. Then color the arrows.

 joints    muscles

3   **Do** Point and say.

I can swim. I use my muscles.

Can you ...
... run?   ... dance?
... throw a ball?   ... swim?   ... play soccer?

Point to the bones, muscles, and joints you use.

I can read and understand about how my body moves.

91

LESSON 9
Project

'About me' poster

Let's review

1 ✏️ **Look and match.**

a

b

1. I can play video games.

2. I can play soccer.

Get ready

2 🎧 7.16 ✏️ **Listen and number. Then say in pairs.**

Sure. It's D-R-A-W. ☐

José, can you help me? How do you spell *draw*? ☐

Thank you! ☐

Workbook page 85

Create

3 🎨 **Now make a poster about you. Write.**

Reflect 😞 🙂 😀

4 How did I do?

I ask for help. ○

I help my friends. ○

I make my project. ○

I can draw and write about what I can do.

92

LESSON 10
Review

1. ✏️ 💬 Circle. Then say.

He can run.

1	2	3	4
throw a ball / play the piano	hop / read	paint / ride a bike	jump rope / run

2. 💬 Look and put a ✔ or ✘ for you. Ask and answer in pairs.

Can you sing?

Yes, I can.

3. 💡 Think and check (✔). Then stick!

I can ...
- 💬 name free time activities ☐
- 📖 read a story ☐
- 🎵 sing a song ☐
- 🧍 keep trying when it's hard ☐

Sticker time

✔ I completed Unit 7!

Go online
Big Project

93

8 My home

living room

Video story

rug

1. Watch the video. Check (✓).

2. Watch again. What does Carl need?

LESSON 1 **Vocabulary**

3 🎧 💬 Listen, find, and say. Then ask a friend.

4 🎵 Listen, chant, and act. 🎵🎵

window

table

I can name things in my home.

Collect your friend! page 5

95

LESSON 2
Vocabulary

1 🎧 💬 **Listen, point, and say. Then play.**

 1 dining room
 2 bedroom
 3 kitchen
 4 bathroom
 5 couch
 6 bed
 7 closet
 8 yard

2 🎧 💬 **Listen and say. Then act and guess.**

 I'm in the …   … bedroom!

3 ✏️ **Find and circle.**

yard / dining room   bedroom / kitchen   bathroom / bed   closet / couch

4 💬 **Play the game.**

Bed.

Bedroom!

Talk buddies

I can name rooms and furniture.

LESSON 3
Grammar

1 🎧 8.5 **Listen and check (✓).**

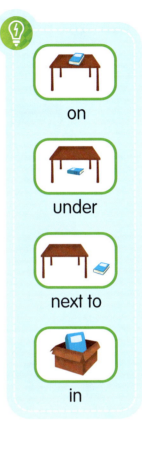
on
under
next to
in

🎧 8.6
Where's the rug? It's in the living room.
Where's the book? It's on the table.

2 🎧 8.7 **Listen and stick.**

3 ✏️ 💬 **Write. Then play *Where's the …?***

Where's the doll?

It's in the _____ .

Where's the robot?

It's ____ the _____ .

I can ask and say where things are.

97

LESSON 4
Story

Where's the ball?

1 🎧 8.8 Listen and read. Does Li need all her toys?

Spot! Can you find a kite?

2 ✏️ **Look, read, and number in order.**

The children can play! The children clean up. Li gives Camila a toy. Li can't find her ball.

3 ✏️ **Read and circle.**

1. What does Li need?

2. The room is clean. How does Li feel?

3. What does Li want to do with the old toys?

4 💬 **Act out the story.**

I don't need this doll.

And you don't need this!

Talk buddies

I can read and understand a story.

99

LESSON 5
Vocabulary

1 🎧 💬 Listen, point, and say. Then play.

1 lamp

2 picture

3 clock

4 wall

5 bookcase

6 shower

Where is it?
shower → bathroom,
clock → bedroom and kitchen

Picture Dictionary
page 126

2 🎧 💬 Listen and say. Then play in pairs.

 It's in the bathroom.

Shower!

Sing-along

3 🎵 Listen, sing, and act.

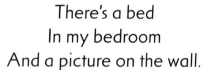

There's a bed
In my bedroom
And a picture on the wall.

There's a robot
In the closet
And a big yellow ball.

I like my bedroom.
I like my bedroom.
It's just for me!

There's a clock
On the bookcase
And a lamp and a TV.

Chorus

I can name things in my home.

LESSON 6
Grammar and Speaking

1 Watch the video. Circle. What can you see in the house?

There's a table.   There are two chairs.
There isn't a TV.   There aren't any toys.

2 Listen and say *Yes* or *No*. Then write.

chairs   bed   lamps   shower

1. There's a _____ .
2. There isn't a _____ .
3. There are two _____ .
4. There aren't any _____ .

Let's communicate!

3 Use the cut outs. Talk with a friend.

There's a picture in the bathroom.

There are two clocks in the kitchen.

I can describe where things are.

LESSON 7
Myself and others

Making decisions

Listen and sing. 1.14

1 🔆 ✏️ Think and match. What don't they need?

doll
pictures
table
chair
dinosaur

2 ✏️ 🎧 Circle what they don't need. Listen and check. 8.14

3 💡 💬 Think and check (✔) for you. Then say.

I don't need this toy.

❋ My bedroom is clean.

❋ My desk is messy.

❋ I can find things I need.

❋ I have toys I don't need.

Be a hero!

What toys don't you need?
Give them to other children.

Responsible decision-making I can make decisions about what I need.

Amazing houses

LESSON 8
My world

1   **Let's explore!** Listen and number.

This window has a lot of triangles and **diamonds**.

The window in this house has four sides. It's a **square**.

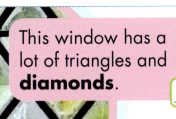

This house is small. It's an **oval**. The windows are ovals, too. But windows can be different shapes.

This window has six sides. It's a **hexagon**.

2   **Think** What shape is it? Say.

   It's an oval!

3 **Do** Design a house with different shapes.

I can read and understand about shapes.

103

**LESSON 9
Project**

My dream bedroom

Let's review

1 🎧 8.16 ✏️ **Listen and check (✓). Then write.**

In my dream bedroom, there's a computer. There are _____ clocks! There's a _____ and a tablet.

Get ready

2 🎧 8.17 ✏️ **Listen and number.**

What's that? ☐

Can you repeat, please? ☐

Raise your hand. ☐

Wait for your turn. ☐

Workbook page 97

Create

3 🎨 💬 Now design your dream bedroom. Then tell the class.

Reflect ☹ 🙂 😀

4 How did I do?

I listen to others. ○

I ask questions. ○

I'm polite. ○

I can design and talk about my dream bedroom.

I can do it!

LESSON 10 Review

1 Circle. Then number. Talk with a friend.

It's the **kitchen** / **living room** / **bedroom** / **bathroom**.

rug
picture
lamp

window
bed
wall

2 Look at 1. Write *Yes* or *No*.

1. There's a couch. _____
2. There are pictures on the wall. _____
3. There's isn't a closet. _____
4. There aren't any books. _____

3 Think and check (✔). Then stick!

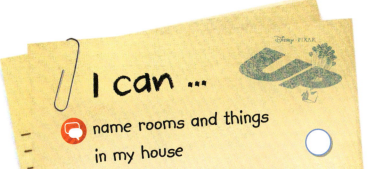

I can ...
- name rooms and things in my house
- read a story
- sing a song
- make decisions about what I need

Sticker time

✔ **I completed Unit 8!**

Go online
Big Project

LESSON 2
Vocabulary

1 🎧 💬 **Listen, point, and say. Then play.**

1. shirt
2. jeans
3. hoodie
4. cap
5. T-shirt
6. shorts
7. sneakers
8. sandals

2 🎧 💬 **Listen and say. Then play in pairs.**

 They're gray.

Jeans!

3 ✏️ **Color and find. Then circle.**

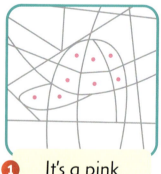 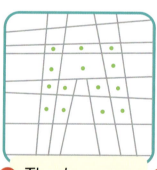 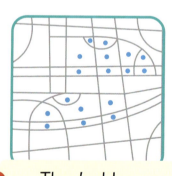 

1. It's a pink **cap** / **hoodie**.
2. They're green **jeans** / **shorts**.
3. They're blue **sneakers** / **sandals**.
4. It's an orange **shirt** / **T-shirt**.

4 💬 **Play the game.** Blue. Sneakers!

108

I can name clothes.

LESSON 3
Grammar

1 🎧 Listen and check (✔).

"I'm wearing a scarf."

🎧 9.6
I'm wearing jeans.   I'm not wearing a dress.
Are you wearing a dress?   Yes, I am.
Are you wearing shorts?   No, I'm not.

2 🎧✏️ Listen and stick. Then write.

 Sticker time

I'm wearing a red _____ .

I'm wearing purple _____ .

3 💬 Play *Guess who?*

Are you wearing a T-shirt?   Yes, I am!

Talk buddies

I can ask and say what I'm wearing.

109

LESSON 4
Story

The lucky cap

1. 🎧 Listen and read. What color is Hugo's cap?

Spot! Can you find Hugo's cap?

2 ✏️ Look, read, and match.

ⓐ She's wearing a purple dress. ⓑ She asks the friends to help. ⓒ He can't find his cap. ⓓ He tells Hugo 'You can do it'.

3 Check (✓). How do the friends help Hugo?

 They hold his hand. ◯

 They play together. ◯

 They give him a toy. ◯

 They give him a hug. ◯

4 💬 Act out the story.

Are you OK, Hugo? Why are you worried?

I can't find my lucky cap.

I can read and understand a story.

LESSON 5
Vocabulary

1 🎧 💬 Listen, point, and say. Then play.

 1 bag

 2 camera

 3 skateboard

 4 paints

 5 markers

 6 building bricks

Make your own picture dictionary. Draw your favorite things.

skateboard

Picture Dictionary page 127

2 🎧 💬 Listen and say. Then play in pairs.

 Is it a camera?

 Yes!

Sing-along

3 🎵 Listen, sing, and act.

I'm wearing my sneakers.
I'm wearing my jeans.
My favorite T-shirt
And my favorite cap!

This is my skateboard.
This is my bag.
This is my camera
And these are my friends.

Smile for the camera.
Smile everyone!
Five, four, three, two, one!

Click!

I can name my things.

Extra Lesson

Go online Phonics

LESSON 6
Grammar and Speaking

1 Watch the video. Circle. Who are Anna's friends?

This is my bag.   These are my books.
Is this your bag?   Yes, it is./No, it isn't.
Are these your books?   Yes, they are./No, they aren't.

2 Listen and number. Then say in pairs.

a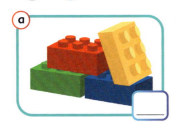
b
c

This is my skateboard.

d
e
f

These are my paints.

Let's communicate!

3 Use the cut outs. Talk with a friend.

I'm wearing shorts.

This is my bag.

These are my sandals.

I can ask and answer about people's things.

113

LESSON 7
Myself and others

Feeling better

1 What makes them feel better? Act out.

2 🎧 Listen and check (✓).

3 💡✏️ Think. What makes you feel better? Read and write.

| my favorite toy   my friend   my favorite clothes   a hug |

❶ When I'm sad, _____ makes me feel better.

❷ When I'm angry, _____ makes me feel better.

✨ Be a hero! ✨

Make a feel better box.
Put your favorite things inside.
Show your friend.

Self-awareness I can say what makes me feel better.

Smart wool!

LESSON 8
My world

1   **Let's explore!** Listen and number.

We make clothes from it! You can wear them when it's hot and cold. I'm wearing a Merino sweater. It's wet outside. But I'm not **wet** or cold. I'm **dry** and warm.

These are Merino **sheep**. They're special! They can live in very **hot** places, and in very **cold** places. The wool from Merino sheep is special, too. It's very soft and light.

sheep

hot

cold

dry

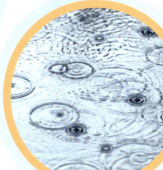
wet

2  **Think** Read and write *Yes* or *No*.

1. Merino wool is from cats. _____
2. The wool is soft and light. _____
3. You can only wear Merino clothes when it's cold. _____

3 Do Put a ✔ or ✘. What can you wear?

	It's hot. ☀	It's cold. ❄	It's wet. 🌧	It's dry. ✘
Merino jacket				
Plastic jacket				

I can read and understand about smart wool.

LESSON 9
Project

My clothes poster

Let's review

1 ✏️ **Read and number.**

a) I'm wearing jeans, a hoodie, and a cap. ☐

b) I'm wearing shorts, a T-shirt, and sneakers. ☐

1

2

Get ready

2 🎧 ✏️ **Listen and number. Then look and match.** 9.16

Draw and color. ☐
Show the class my picture. ☐
Read and check my work. ☐
Get my things ready. ☐
Think and plan! ☐
Write about my picture. ☐

 a
 b
 c
 d
 e
 f

Workbook page 109

Create

3 🎨 Now design your clothes. Write.

Reflect 🙂 🙁 😁

4 How did I do?

I think and plan.

I create my project.

I can design and write about my clothes.

I can do it!

LESSON 10 Review

1   Circle. Then say for you.

I'm wearing shorts.

shirt / bag   shirt / sweater   jacket / boots   shorts / dress

2  Listen and put a ✓ or ✗. Then ask and answer.

Is this your camera?

No, it isn't.

3 Think and check (✓). Then stick!

Sticker time

I can ...
- name my clothes and things ☐
- read a story ☐
- sing a song ☐
- say what makes me feel better ☐

Test your progress with English Benchmark Young Learners

✓ **I completed Unit 9!**

Go online Big Project

117

W

1 Find and stick. **2** Listen, point, and say. **3** Trace.

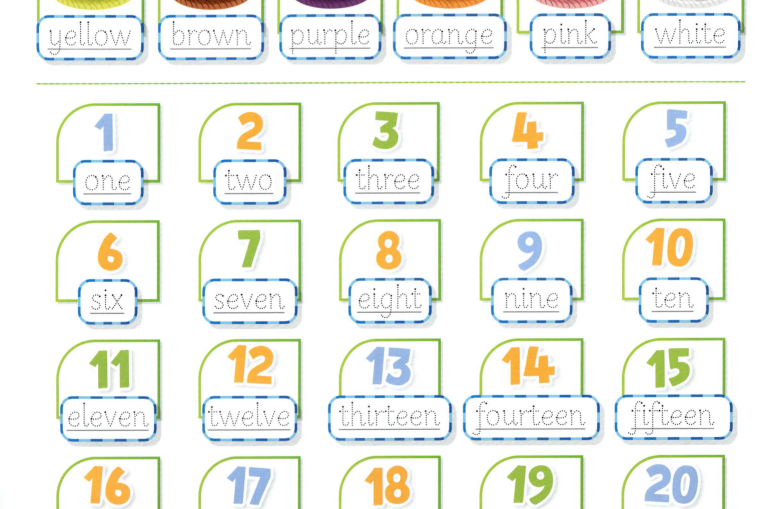

1 Find and stick. 2 Listen, point, and say. 3 Trace.
4 Circle your school things. Then draw your pencil case.

classroom
teacher

student
desk

Sticker time

 book
 backpack
 pencil
 pen

 chair
 board
 poster
 door

 crayon
 eraser
 ruler

 pencil case
big
small

119

1 Find and stick. **2** Listen, point, and say. **3** Trace.
4 Big or small? Write for you.

Sticker time

dad
brother
mom
sister

 big sister
 baby brother
 grandpa
 grandma

 aunt
 uncle
 cousin
 friend

 boy
 girl
 young

 old
 nice
 funny

big

small

3

1. Find and stick.   2. Listen, point, and say.   3. Trace.
4. Draw your face and label.

body · head · leg · arm

 face
 eye
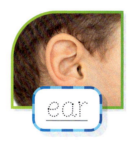 ear
 nose

 mouth
 hair
 hand
 finger

 sit down
 stand up
 listen

 show
 open
 close

4

 1 Find and stick. **2** Listen, point, and say. **3** Trace.
4 How many legs? Write.

bird
cat
dog
hamster

 mouse  fish  rabbit  frog

 turtle  lizard  snake  horse

 duck  fox  squirrel

 spider  ant  bee

bee – _____ legs
duck – _____ legs
horse – _____ legs
snake – _____ legs
spider – _____ legs

1 Find and stick. **2** Listen, point, and say. **3** Write.
4 One word or two words?

action figure   dinosaur   doll   toys

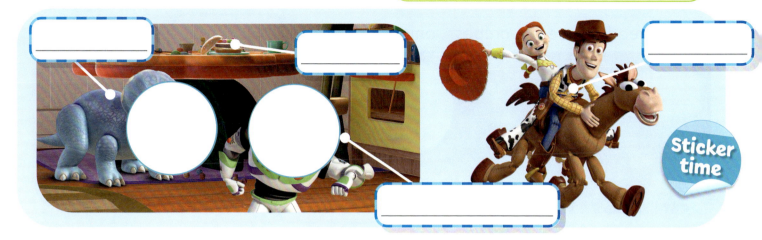

Sticker time

ball   car   kite
new   plane   robot
teddy bear   train

One word

Two words

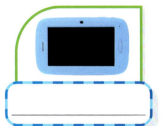

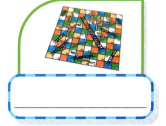

board game   scooter
tablet   tennis racket
TV   watch

123

1 Find and stick. **2** Listen, point, and say. **3** Write.
4 Circle food that you like. Then draw one more.

bread   cheese   grapes   onions

Sticker time

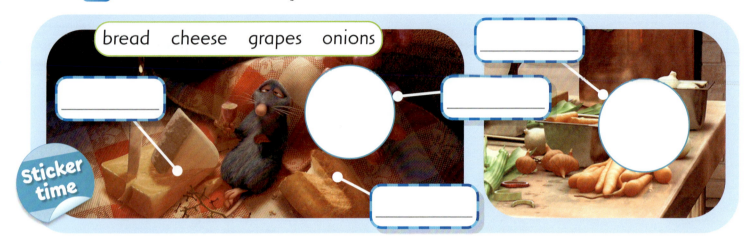

bananas   carrots
eggs   juice   milk
oranges   pears
tomatoes

fruit   jam   meat
pasta   pie   rice

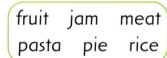

7

1 Find and stick.   **2** Listen, point, and say.   **3** Write.

4 Which actions use a ball? | dance   paint   play the guitar   read |

Sticker time

| catch a ball |
| jump rope |
| play soccer |
| play video games |
| ride a bike   run |
| sing   throw a ball |

| bounce a ball   draw |
| hop   play the piano |
| swim   use a computer |

125

8

1. Find and stick.   2.  Listen, point, and say.   3. Write.
4. Draw a room in your house. What's in it? Circle.

living room
rug   table
window

bathroom   bed
bedroom   closet
couch   dining room
kitchen   yard

clock   bookcase   lamp
picture   shower   wall

9

1 Find and stick. **2** 🎧 Listen, point, and say. **3** ✏️ Write.
4 What do you wear ...?

boots   dress   jacket   sweater

cap   hoodie   jeans
sandals   shirt   shorts
sneakers   T-shirt

top

bottom

bag   building bricks
camera   markers
paints   skateboard

Pearson Education Limited
KAO Two
KAO Park
Hockham Way
Harlow, Essex
CM17 9SR
England
and Associated Companies throughout the world.

pearsonenglish.com
© Pearson Education Limited 2022

© 2022 Disney Enterprises, Inc. All rights reserved. Pixar properties © Disney/Pixar

Materials and characters from the movie Cars. Copyright © 2022 Disney Enterprises, Inc. and Pixar. All rights reserved. Disney/Pixar elements ©Disney/Pixar; rights in underlying vehicles are the property of the following third parties, as applicable: Porsche is a trademark of Porsche. Plymouth Superbird is a trademark of FCA US U.C. Petty marks used by permissions of Petty Marketing LLC. Mercury is a trademark of Ford Motor Company.

The term OMNIDROID used by permission of Lucasfilm Ltd.

Mr. and Mrs. Potato Head® are registered trademarks of Hasbro, Inc. Used with permission. © Hasbro, Inc. All rights reserved. © Just Play, LLC.

The right of Tessa Lochowski to be identified as author of this Work has been asserted by her in accordance with the Copyright, Designs and Patents Act 1988.

All rights reserved; no part of this publication may be reproduced, stored in a retrieval system, or transmitted in any form or by any means, electronic, mechanical, photocopying, recording, or otherwise without the prior written permission of the Publishers.

First published 2022
ISBN: 978-1-292-44158-0
Set in Arta Medium 19/25pt

Printed in Slovakia by Neografia

Acknowledgements
The publishers and author would like to thank the following people for their feedback and comments during the development of the material: Maria Silvina Campagnoli, Maria Lidia Camporro, Maria Sol Diaz, Tatiana Fanshtein, Jiang Xin, Paula Mior, Anita Parlaj-Naranic, Marta Popiolek, Jelena Tosic.

Image Credits
123RF.com: 5second 30, 32, Belchonock 84, 125, Dean Drobot 41, Iriana88w 96, 126, Katarzyna Białasiewicz 100, 126, Lily Oh 104, Paolo De Santis 12, Pat138241 20, 76, Sam74100 88, 100, Sasin Tipchai 48, 122, Thomas Perkins 114, Vyacheslav Volkov 114, Wabeno 64, 123; **Alamy Stock Photo:** IMAGEMORE Co. Ltd 68, Pixel-shot 60, 123, Stan Pritchard 103; **Getty Images:** 3bugsmom 64, Aabejon 28, Aluxum 76, 124, AndreaObzerova 100, Annebaek 89, Baona 28, BeylaBalla 108, 127, Borisyankov 12, Creative Crop 64, 123, Dan Totilca 12, David Madison 84, 93, 125, Diane Labombarbe 12, Erikreis 24, FatCamera 19, 53, 80, 104, FollowTheFlow 100, 126, Fran Polito 88, 93, 125, Fstop123 19, Ghislain & Marie David de Lossy 67, GlobalStock 84, HappyKids 44, Hill Street Studios 31, Hocus-focus 100, Image Source 114, Imgorthand 90, Inti St. Clair 90, Isabel Pavia 73, Jaroon 15, 17, 29, JBryson 16, 25, JGI/Jamie Grill 54, 67, JohnnyGreig 88, 125, Jonathan Kirn 61, Jose Luis Pelaez Inc 25, 30, 78, 84, 88, 93, 93, 125, 125, Khosrork 112, Kool99 15, 27, Kwangmoozaa 72, 124, Lane Oatey/Blue Jean Images 61, 65, 113, LightFieldStudios 60, 77, 123, Loco75 102, Lupengyu 103, Manonallard 80, Marc Romanelli 32, Maskot 78, MBI 31, Mehmet Özhan Araboga / EyeEm 48, 122, Melpomenem 60, 123, MonstArrr_ 96, Narisara Nami 109, Natikka 12, Nattanapong 67, Photo by Rafa Elias 42, Plan Shoot / Imazins 72, Poco_bw 61, Princessdlaf 63, Prostock-Studio 80, Pskeltonphoto 52, 122, Rafita Images 88, SergiyN 113, Serhiy Hlupak 48, 122, Sirikorn Thamniyom / EyeEm 87, Sturti 30, Suparat Malipoom / EyeEm 72, 124, Taek-sang Jeong 108, 127, Tetra Images - Daniel Grill 30, TorriPhoto 52, 122, Tuomonws 66, 88, 125, Vstock LLC 104, Wavebreakmedia 19, 52, 99, Westend61 76, 79, 92, 124, Zheka-Boss 51, Ziggy_mars 84, 125; **Pearson Education Ltd:** Jon Barlow 5, Trevor Clifford 65, 101; **Shutterstock:** 5 second Studio 36, 121, ABO PHOTOGRAPHY 111, Adisa 108, 127, Africa Studio 27, 72, 76, 84, 96, 116, 124, 125, 126, Alinute Silzeviciute 115, Amenic181 79, Anastasiia Guseva 43, Anatoliy Karlyuk 42, 75, 76, Andrey Pavlov. 52, 122, Anna Yunak 103, Annashou 114, Anneka 48, 122, ANURAK PONGPATIMET 39, ArCaLu 115, Arek_malang 88, 125, Artazum 96, 126, Artazum and Iriana Shiyan 96, 126, Artem Samokhvalov 12, Beata Becla 43, BERNATSKAIA OKSANA 36, 121, BestPhotoStudio 115, BigPixel Photo 40, 121, Black-Photogaphy 36, 121, Bqmeng 112, 127, Brian A Jackson 90, Drillenstimmer 43, Christian Delbert 12, Cookie Studio 24, Creativestockexchange 20, DarvidArt 16, Dave Pot 16, 76, Denis Kovin 67, Dipak Shelare 84, Dmitrii Dektiarev 103, Dmitrii Pridannikov 96, 126, Dmitry Lobanov 54, 66, Drpnncpptak 103, Elliotte Rusty Harold 52, 122, ESOlex 112, 127, ESTUDI M6 52, Eurobanks 36, 36, 121, 121, Fotohunter 79, Fotokon 103, Fotokostic 79, Fuller Photography 16, Gelpi 36, 77, 96, 121, Gemenacom 63, Gladskikh Tatiana 61, GOLFX 29, 64, 75, 89, 112, Graystock 43, Greenland 84, 125, Gregory Johnston 115, Grigorita Ko 55, GUNDAM_Ai 37, Here 52, Hogan Imaging 101, Iofoto 41, Jay Ondreicka 48, 122, Jesterpop 60, 123, JGade 39, John Carnemolla 115, JR-50 80, Jstengel 48, 122, Just dance 114, Kiattipong 100, 126, KK Tan 78, Kongsky 103, Kornnphoto 54, Kustomer 108, 127, Kuvona 76, 124, Lammotos 40, 121, Lanych 92, LELACHANOK SANGUANRAKSAK 72, 124, LeNi 20, Leyla Ismet 72, 124, LianeM 52, 122, Lifestyle Travel Photo 72, 108, 124, 127, LightField Studios 36, 64, Lillac 48, 122, Littlekidmoment 40, 43, 121, Ljupco Smokovski 64, 123, Lopolo 36, 40, 48, 99, 108, 121, Lorelyn Medina 17, Luca Santilli 76, 124, Luchschen 100, 126, Luis Molinero 111, Mar1Art1 12, Marharyta Gangalo 40, Marlinda vd Spek 55, Marlon Lopez MMG1 Design 66, Maryna Pleshkun 65, 79, Maximilian100 88, 125, MBI 19, 31, 31, 43, 56, Mega Pixel 16, 112, 127, Mihalec 20, Momoforsale 112, 127, Mr Twister 115, MVelishchuk 64, 123, Mydegage 72, 124, MyImages - Micha 60, 123, Naluwan 44, Natalia Lebedinskaia 79, Nataliya Dorokhina 43, Nazarovsergey 77, Neirfy 96, 126, New Africa 96, 126, Nickola_Che 79, Ninell Creative 79, Oleg_Mit 103, Oleksandr Shatyrov 67, Panatda Saengow 67, Parinya Binsuk 48, Paul B. Moore 88, PCHT 55, Peter Vanco 67, Photodiem 67, Photographee.eu 100, 100, 126, 126, Picsfive 16, Piotr Sikora 60, 123, Pixfiction 108, 127, PongMoji 43, Posteriori 108, 127, Pressmaster 40, 121, PrimaStockPhoto 16, Prostock-studio 42, Rawpixel.com 51, RAYphotographer 103, RimDream 42, Rita_Kochmarjova 48, 122, Rob Marmion 84, 125, S-F 18, Saaras 96, 126, Sandra Standbridge 52, 122, Sergei Kolesnikov 56, 66, Sergiy Bykhunenko 68, sevenke 103, Shebeko 72, 124, ShotPrime Studio 87, Skazka Grez 64, 123, Spass 40, 121, Stockfour 80, StockImageFactory.com 39, Stopabox 36, 121, Supertrooper 60, 123, Suti Stock Photo 20, Taelove7 112, 127, Tatiana Popova 67, TheFarAwayKingdom 112, 127, TheVisualsYouNeed 84, 112, 125, Time4studio 64, 123, Tnehala77 20, Tom Bird 115, Tomaz Plut 20, Trattieritratti 91, TY Lim 42, 54, Vania Zhukevych 76, 124, Vasyliuk 60, 123, Vitaly Zorkin 20, Vladvm 16, Wavebreakmedia 28, 40, 108, 121, Weerastudio 79, Wiktory 72, 124, WildMedia 55, Xiaorui 108, 127, Yevgeniy11 55, Ziggy_mars 43.

Cover images © 2022 Disney Enterprises, Inc. All rights reserved. Pixar properties © Disney/Pixar

All other images © Pearson Education

Illustrations
Anna Bishop/Advocate: pp.21, 24, 48, 55 (activity 3), 60, 72, 102 (activity 2);
Emily Cooksey/Plum Pudding: (doodles), pp.16, 20 (activity 1), 32, 44, 56 (activity 1), 68 (activity 1), 80, 93, 104, 112, 116 (activity 1); **Dean Gray/Advocate:** (cutouts), pp.12, 13, 19 (activity 3), 49, 61, 77, 84, 91 (activity 2), 108, 115; **Sejung Kim/Advocate:** pp.55 (activity 2), 66 (activity 3), 73, 90, 96, 101, 113; **Jessica Martinello/Plum Pudding:** pp.25, 41 (activity 2), 53, 57, 78 (activity 2), 89, 97 (activity 2), 109, 116 (activity 2), 117; **Marisa Morea/Plum Pudding: (course characters); Diego Vaisberg/Advocate:** pp.6, 41 (activity 1), 42 (activity 3), 43, 54 (activity 3), 91 (activity 1), 97 (activity 1).

Unit 1

Cut outs

Unit 2

Cut outs

Unit 3

Unit 4

Cut outs

Unit 5

Cut outs

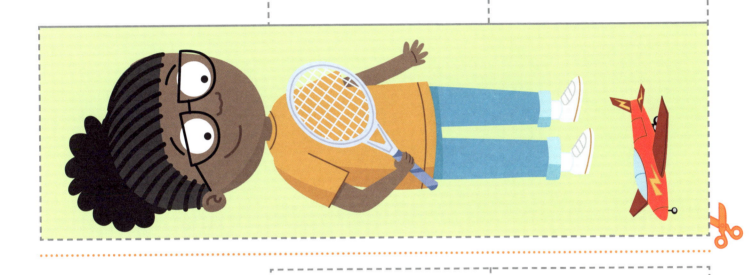

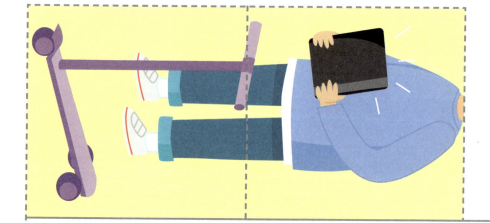

Unit 6

Cut outs

Unit 7

Unit 8

Cut outs

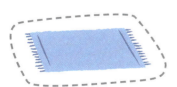

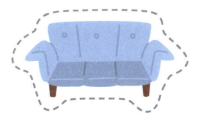

Unit 9

Cut outs